THE ~~BIBLE ON~~

Scriptures s~

MW00490736

INTRODUCTION

When I read these Bible verses, my mind is filled with praise
and soon overflows with joy. Deep within, I sense my spirit
responding in worship to God. I keep my copy of *The Bible on Praise*
where I can devour it daily. My mind is repeatedly
refreshed, revived and my entire body responds in new health
and gladness. I strongly recommend that you read these verses at
least once each week. Many blessings come to those who praise Him.

Scriptures in *The Bible on Praise* are in the King James
Version, except where noted.

ISBN 0-943026-03-2
Copyright © 1981
Merlin R.Carothers
PO Box 2518
Escondido,CA 92033
www.merlincarothers.com
Printed in the USA

THE BIBLE ON PRAISE

EXODUS

15:1 Then sang Moses and the children of
Israel this song unto the Lord, and spake, saying, I will
sing unto the Lord, for he hath triumphed gloriously …

DEUTERONOMY

8:10 Thou shalt bless the Lord
thy God for the good land which he hath given thee.

II SAMUEL

22:4 I will call on the Lord, who is worthy
to be praised: so shall I be saved from mine enemies.
50 Therefore I will give thanks unto thee, O Lord
among the heathen, and I will sing praises unto thy name.

I KINGS

8:56 Blessed be the Lord, that hath given rest
unto his people … according to all that he promised:
there hath not failed one word of all his good promises,
which he promised …

I CHRONICLES

16:8 Give thanks unto the Lord,
call upon his name, make known his deeds among the people.
9 Sing unto him, sing psalms
unto him, talk ye of all of his wondrous works.
10 Glory ye in his holy name:
let the heart of them rejoice that seek the Lord.
23 Sing unto the Lord, all the
earth; shew forth from day to day his salvation.
24 Declare his glory among the heathen;
his marvelous works among all nations.
25 For great is the Lord, and greatly to be praised …
29 Give unto the Lord the glory due
unto his name: bring an offering, and come before him:
worship the Lord in the beauty of holiness.
31 Let the heavens be glad, and let
the earth rejoice: and let men say among the nations,
the Lord reigneth.
32 Let the sea roar, and the fullness
thereof: let the fields rejoice, and all that is therein.
34 O give thanks unto the Lord;
for he is good; for his mercy endureth forever.
35 And say ye, Save us, O God of
our salvation, and gather us together, and deliver us
from the heathen, that we may give thanks to
thy holy name, and glory in thy praise.

36 Blessed be the Lord God of Israel
for ever and ever. And all the people said, Amen,
and praised the Lord.
29:11 Thine, O Lord, is the greatness,
and the power, and the glory, and the victory, and the
majesty: for all that is in the heaven and in the earth
is thine; thine is the kingdom, O Lord, and
thou art exalted as head above all.
13 Now therefore, our God,
we thank thee, and praise thy glorious name.
20 And David said to all the congregation,
Now bless the Lord your God. And all the congregation
blessed the Lord God of their fathers, and
bowed down their heads and worshipped the Lord …

II CHRONICLES

5:13 It came even to pass, as the trumpeters
and singers were as one, to make one sound to be heard
in praising and thanking the Lord;
and when they lifted up their voice with the trumpets
and cymbals and instruments of music, and praised the
Lord, saying … For he is good; for his mercy
endureth for ever: that then the house was filled
with a cloud, even the house of the Lord:
14 So that the priests could not stand to
minister by reason of the cloud: for the glory of the
Lord had filled the house of God.

7:3 And when all the children of Israel
saw how the fire came down, and the glory of the Lord
upon the house, they bowed themselves with their faces
to the ground upon the pavement, and worshipped,
and praised the Lord, saying, For he is good;
for his mercy endureth for ever.
20:21 And when he had consulted with the people,
he appointed singers unto the Lord ... that should praise
the beauty of holiness, as they went out
before the army, and to say, praise the Lord,
for his mercy endureth for ever.

*When the army was preceded by the praise choir,
the enemy was confused and destroyed.*

NEHEMIAH

8:10 ...This day is holy unto
our Lord: ... the joy of the Lord is your strength.

*The secret of how to obtain **new** strength.*

9:5 ... Stand up and bless the Lord
your God for ever and ever: and blessed be thy glorious
name, which is exalted above all blessing and praise.

6 Thou, even thou, art Lord alone; thou
hast made heaven, the heaven of heavens, with all their
host, the earth, and all things that are therein, the seas,
and all that is therein, and thou preservest them all;
and the host of heaven worshippeth thee.

*Prayer: Let us praise You, O Lord, forever and ever.
Let our words and thoughts be more and more
filled with praise.*

12:43 ... That day they offered great sacrifices,
and rejoiced: for God had made them rejoice
with great joy: the wives also and the children rejoiced:
so that the joy of Jerusalem was heard even afar off.

JOB

1:21 … Naked came I out of my mother's womb,
and naked shall I return thither: the Lord gave, and the
Lord hath taken away; blessed be the name of the Lord.
8:21 Till he fill thy mouth with
laughing, and thy lips with rejoicing.
38:7 When the morning stars sang
together, and all the sons of God shouted for joy.

PSALMS

5:11 But let all those that put their trust
in thee rejoice: let them ever shout for joy, because
thou defendest them: let them also that love
thy name be joyful in thee.

7:17 I will praise the Lord according to
his righteousness: and will sing praise to the name
of the Lord most high.

9:1 I will praise thee, O Lord, with my
whole heart; I will shew forth all thy marvelous works.

2 I will be glad and rejoice in thee: I will sing praise to thy name,
O thou most High.

14 That I may shew forth all thy praise …
I will rejoice in thy salvation.

13:6 I will sing unto the Lord,
because he hath dealt bountifully with me.

16:8 I have set the Lord always before me:
because he is at my right hand, I shall not be moved.

9 Therefore my heart is glad, and my glory
rejoiceth: my flesh also shall rest in hope.

11 Thou wilt shew me the path of life:
in thy presence is fulness of joy; at thy right hand
there are pleasures for evermore.

18:2 The Lord is my rock, and my fortress, and
my deliverer; my God, my strength, in whom I will trust …

49 Therefore will I give thanks unto thee, O Lord,
among the heathen, and sing praises unto thy name.

19:1 The heavens declare the glory of God;
and the firmament sheweth his handiwork.
20:5 We will rejoice in thy salvation,
and in the name of our God we will set up our banners ...
21:1 The king shall joy in thy strength, O Lord;
and in thy salvation how greatly shall he rejoice!
13 Be thou exalted, Lord, in thine
own strength: so will we sing and praise thy power.
22:3 But thou art holy, O thou
that inhabits the praises of Israel.
26 The meek shall eat and be satisfied:
they shall praise the Lord that seek him.
27:6 ... I offer in his tabernacle
sacrifices of joy; I will sing, yea, I will sing
praises unto the Lord.
28:7 The Lord is my strength and my shield; my
heart trusted in him, and I am helped: therefore my heart
greatly rejoiceth; and with my song will I praise him.
29:2 Give unto the Lord the glory due
unto his name; worship the Lord in the beauty of holiness.
30:4 Sing unto the Lord, O ye saints of his,
and give thanks at the remembrance of his holiness.
5 ... Weeping may endure for
a night, but joy cometh in the morning.
11 Thou hast turned for me my mourning
into dancing: thou hast put off my sackcloth,
and girded me with gladness;

12 To the end that my glory may sing praise
to thee, and not be silent. O Lord my God, I will give
thanks unto thee for ever.
33:21 ... Our heart shall rejoice
in him, because we have trusted in his holy name.
34:1 I will bless the Lord at all times:
his praise shall continually be in my mouth.
2 My soul shall make her boast
in the Lord: the humble shall hear thereof, and be glad.
3 O magnify the Lord with me,
and let us exalt his name together.
35:9 And my soul shall be joyful
in the Lord: it shall rejoice in his salvation.
18 I will give thee thanks in the great
congregation: I will praise thee among much people.
28 And my tongue shall speak of
thy righteousness and of thy praise all the day long.

The Bible says that David was "a man after God's own heart."

40:3 And he hath put a new song in my mouth,
even praise unto our God: many shall see it, and fear,
and shall trust in the Lord.
16 Let all those that seek thee rejoice
and be glad in thee: let such as love thy salvation
say continually, The Lord be magnified.
41:13 Blessed be the Lord God of Israel
from everlasting, and to everlasting. Amen, and Amen.

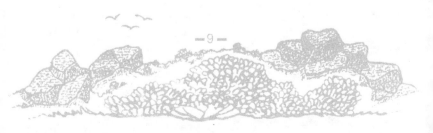

43:5 Why art thou cast down, O my soul?
and why art thou disquieted in me? hope in God:
for I shall yet praise him, for the
health of his countenance, and my God.
44:8 In God we boast all the day
long, and praise thy name forever.
47:1 Clap your hands, all ye people;
shout unto God with the voice of triumph.
6 Sing praises to God, sing praises:
sing praises unto our King, sing praises.
7 For God is the King of all
the earth: sing ye praises with understanding.
48:1 Great is the Lord, and greatly to be praised
in the city of our God, in the mountain of his holiness.
2 Beautiful for situation, the joy
of the whole earth, is Mount Zion, on the sides
of the north, the city of the great King.
10 According to thy name, O God,
so is thy praise unto the ends of the earth:
thy right hand is full of righteousness.
50:14 Offer unto God thanksgiving;
and pay thy vows unto the most High:
15 And call upon me in the day of trouble:
I will deliver thee, and thou shalt glorify me.
23 Whoso offereth praise glorifieth me:
and to him that ordereth his conversation
aright will I shew the salvation of God.

57:5 Be thou exalted, O God, above
the heavens; let thy glory be above all the earth.
7 My heart is fixed, O God,
my heart is fixed: I will sing and give praise.
63:3 Because thy lovingkindness
is better than life, my lips shall praise thee.
4 Thus will I bless thee while
I live: I will lift up my hands in thy name.
5 My soul shall be satisfied as with marrow and
fatness; and my mouth shall praise thee with joyful lips:
6 When I remember thee upon my bed,
and meditate on thee in the night watches.
7 Because thou hast been my help,
therefore in the shadow of thy wings will I rejoice.
66:1 Make a joyful noise unto God, all ye lands:
2 Sing forth the honour of
his name: make his praise glorious.
8 Bless our God, ye people,
and make the voice of his praise to be heard.
67:3 Let the people praise thee,
O God; let all the people praise thee.
4 O let the nations be glad and
sing for joy: for thou shalt judge the people righteously,
and govern the nations upon earth.
68:3 … Let the righteous be glad; let them
rejoice before God: yea, let them exceedingly rejoice.

32 Sing unto God, ye kingdoms of
the earth; O sing praises unto the Lord.
69:30 I will praise the name of God
with a song, and will magnify him with thanksgiving.
34 Let the heaven and earth praise him,
the seas, and everything that moveth therein.
70:4 Let all those that seek thee rejoice
and be glad in thee: and let such as love thy salvation
say continually, Let God be magnified.
71:6 By thee have I been holden up from the womb ...
my praise shall be continually of thee.
8 Let my mouth be filled with
thy praise and with thy honour all the day.
23 My lips shall greatly rejoice when I
sing unto thee; and my soul, which thou hast redeemed.
72:18 Blessed be the Lord God, the God
of Israel, who only doeth wondrous things.
19 And blessed be his glorious name forever: and let
the whole earth be filled with his glory; Amen, and Amen.
75:1 Unto thee, O God, do we give thanks,
unto thee do we give thanks: for that thy name is near
thy wondrous works declare.

79:13 So we thy people and sheep of thy pasture
will give thee thanks forever: we will shew forth thy
praise to all generations.

86:12 I will praise thee, O Lord my God, with
all my heart: and I will glorify thy name for evermore.

89:15 Blessed is the people that know the joyful sound ...

16 In thy name shall they rejoice all the day ...

17 For thou art the glory of their strength.

92:1 It is a good thing to give thanks unto
the Lord, and to sing praises unto thy name, O most High.

95: 1 O come, let us sing unto the Lord:
let us make a joyful noise to the rock of our salvation.

2 Let us come before his presence with
thanksgiving, and make a joyful noise unto him with psalms.

97:12 Rejoice in the Lord, ye righteous,
and give thanks at the remembrance of his holiness.

98:4 Make a joyful noise unto the Lord, all
the earth: make a loud noise, and rejoice, and sing praise.

7 Let the sea roar, and the fullness
thereof; the world, and they that dwell therein.

8 Let the floods clap their hands:
let the hills be joyful together.

100:1 Make a joyful noise unto the Lord, all ye lands.

2 Serve the Lord with gladness:
come before his presence with singing.

3 Know ye that the Lord he is God: it is he
that hath made us, and not we ourselves; we are his people,
and the sheep of his pasture.
4 Enter into his gates with thanksgiving,
and into his courts with praise; be thankful unto him,
and bless his name.
102:18 This shall be written for
the generation to come: and the people which shall
be created shall praise the Lord.
103:1 Bless the Lord, O my soul:
and all that is within me, bless his holy name.
2 Bless the Lord, O my soul,
and forget not all his benefits:
3 Who forgiveth all thine
iniquities; who healeth all thy diseases.
104:1 Bless the Lord, O my soul. O Lord my God, thou
art very great; thou art clothed with honour and majesty.
33 I will sing unto the Lord as long as I
live: I will sing praise to my God while I have my being.
34 My meditation of him shall be
sweet: I will be glad in the Lord.
105:3 Glory ye in his holy name:
let the heart of them rejoice that seek the Lord.
107: 8 Oh that men would praise the Lord
for his goodness, and for his wonderful works
to the children of men!
9 For he satisfieth the longing soul,
and filleth the hungry soul with goodness.

22 And let them sacrifice the sacrifices
of thanksgiving, and declare his works with rejoicing.
108:1 O God, my heart is
fixed; I will sing and give praise …
5 Be thou exalted, O God, above
the heavens: and thy glory above all the earth.
109:30 I will greatly praise the Lord
with my mouth; yea, I will praise him among the multitude.
111:1 Praise ye the Lord. I will praise
the Lord with my whole heart, in the assembly
of the upright, and in the congregation.
113:2 Blessed be the name of
the Lord from this time forth and for evermore.
3 From the rising of the sun unto
the going down of the same the Lord's name is to be praised.
115:1 Not unto us, O Lord, not unto us, but unto thy
name give glory, for thy mercy, and for thy truth's sake.
18 … We will bless the Lord from
this time forth and for evermore. Praise the Lord.
116:12 What shall I render unto
the Lord for all his benefits toward me?
17 I will offer to thee the sacrifice of thanksgiving.
117:1 O praise the Lord,
all ye nations: praise him, all ye people.
2 For his merciful kindness is great
toward us: and the truth of the Lord endureth for ever.
Praise ye the Lord.

118:1 O give thanks unto the Lord;
for he is good: because his mercy endureth for ever.
19 Open to me the gates of righteousness:
I will go into them, and I will praise the Lord:
21 I will praise thee: for thou
hast heard me, and art become my salvation.
24 This is the day which the Lord
hath made; we will rejoice and be glad in it.
28 Thou art my God, and I will
praise thee: thou art my God, I will exalt thee.
29 O give thanks unto the Lord;
for he is good: for his mercy endureth for ever.
119:62 At midnight I will rise to give thanks unto thee …
126:2 Then was our mouth filled with
laughter, and our tongue with singing: then said they among
the heathen, the Lord hath donegreat things for them.
3 The Lord hath done
great things for us; whereof we are glad.
134:2 Lift up your hands
in the sanctuary, and bless the Lord.
135:3 Praise the Lord; for the Lord
is good: sing praises unto his name; for it is pleasant.
138:4 All the kings of the earth shall praise
thee, O Lord, when they hear the words of thy mouth.
5 Yea, they shall sing in the ways
of the Lord: for great is the glory of the Lord.

139:14 I will praise thee; for I am
fearfully and wonderfully made: marvelous are thy works;
and that my soul knoweth right well.
140:13 Surely the righteous shall give thanks
unto thy name: the upright shall dwell in thy presence.
145:2 Every day will I bless thee;
and I will praise thy name for ever and ever ...
3 Great is the Lord, and greatly
to be praised; and his greatness is unsearchable.
5 I will speak of the glorious
honour of thy majesty, and of thy wondrous works.
10 All thy works shall praise thee,
O Lord; and thy saints shall bless thee.
21 My mouth shall speak the praise
of the Lord: and let all flesh bless his holy name
for ever and ever.
146:2 While I live will I praise the Lord:
I will sing praises unto my God while I have any being.
147:1 Praise ye the Lord:
for it is good to sing praises unto our God; for it is
pleasant; and praise is comely.
7 Sing unto the Lord with
thanksgiving; sing praise upon the harp unto our God.
148:2 Praise ye him,
all his angels: praise ye him, all his hosts.

3 Praise ye him,
sun and moon: praise him, all ye stars of light.
4 Praise him, ye heavens
of heavens, and ye waters that be above the heavens.
5 Let them praise the name
of the Lord: for he commanded, and they were created.
12 Both young men,
and maidens; old men, and children:
13 Let them praise
the name of the Lord: for his name alone is excellent;
his glory is above the earth and heaven.
149:3 Let them praise his name in the dance:
let them sing praises unto him with the timbrel and harp.
4 For the Lord taketh pleasure
in his people: he will beautify the meek with salvation.
5 Let the saints be joyful
in glory: let them sing aloud upon their beds.
6 Let the high praises of God
be in their mouth, and a two-edged sword in their hand.

Our praises to God are POWERFUL!

150:2 Praise him for his mighty acts:
praise him according to his excellent greatness.
6 Let everything that hath
breath praise the Lord. Praise ye the Lord.

PROVERBS

15:13 A merry heart maketh a cheerful countenance.
15 ... He that is of a merry heard hath a continual feast.
17:22 A merry heart doeth good
like a medicine: but a broken spirit drieth the bones.

ISAIAH

6:3 And one cried unto another,
and said, Holy, holy, holy, is the Lord of hosts:
the whole earth is full of his glory.
12:1And in that day thou shalt say,
O Lord, I will praise thee: though thou wast angry with
me, thine anger is turned away, and thou comfortedst me.
3 Therefore with joy shall ye
draw water out of the wells of salvation.
4 And in that day shall ye say,
Praise the Lord, call upon his name, declare his doings
among the people, make mention that his name is exalted.
5 Sing unto the Lord; for he
hath done excellent things: this is known in all the earth.
24:14 They shall lift up their voice,
they shall sing for the majesty of the Lord,
they shall cry aloud from the sea.

15 Wherefore glorify ye the Lord
in the fires, even the name of the Lord God of Israel
in the isles of the sea.

29:19 The meek also shall increase their
joy in the Lord, and the poor among men shall rejoice
in the Holy One of Israel.

35:10 And the ransomed of the Lord
shall return, and come to Zion with songs and everlasting
joy upon their heads: they shall obtain joy and gladness,
and sorrow and sighing shall flee away.

43:21 This people have I formed
for myself; they shall shew forth my praise.

49:13 Sing, O heavens; and be joyful,
O earth; and break forth into singing, O mountains:
for the Lord hath comforted his people, and will have
mercy upon his afflicted.

55:12 For ye shall go out with joy,
and be led forth with peace: the mountains and the hills
shall break forth before you into singing, and all the
trees of the field shall clap their hands.

61:11 For as the earth bringeth forth her bud,
and as the garden causeth the things that are sown in it
to spring forth; so the Lord will cause righteousness
and praise to spring forth before all the nations.

JEREMIAH

17:14 Heal me, O Lord, and I shall be healed;
save me, and I shall be saved: for thou art my praise.
30:19 And out of them shall proceed
thanksgiving and the voice of them that make merry.
33:11 The voice of joy, and the voice
of gladness, the voice of the bridegroom, and the voice
of the bride, the voice of them that shall say,
Praise the Lord of hosts: for the Lord is good; for his
mercy endureth for ever: and of them that shall bring the
sacrifice of praise into the house of the Lord.

LAMENTATIONS

3:41 Let us lift up our heart
with our hands unto God in the heavens.

EZEKIEL

3:12 Then the spirit took me up,
and I heard behind me a voice of a great rushing,
saying, Blessed be the glory of the Lord …

DANIEL

2:20 … Blessed be the name of God
for ever and ever: for wisdom and might are his.
4:37 Now I Nebuchadnezzar praise and extol
and honour the King of heaven, all whose works are truth,
and his ways judgment: and those that walk in pride
he is able to abase.

JOEL

2:26 … shall eat in plenty,
and be satisfied, and praise the name of the Lord your
God, that hath dealt wondrously with you: and my people
shall never be ashamed.

JONAH

2:9 But I will sacrifice unto thee with the voice
of thanksgiving; I will pay that that I have vowed.
Salvation is of the Lord.

HABKKUK

3:3 … His glory covered the
heavens, and the earth was full of his praise.
18 … I will rejoice in
the Lord, I will joy in the God of my salvation.

ZEPHANIAH

3:14 ... be glad and rejoice with all the heart ...
17 The Lord thy God in the midst
of thee is mighty; he will save, he will rejoice over thee
with joy; he will rest in his love, he will joy
over thee with singing.

ZECHARIAH

2:10 Sing and rejoice … for, lo, I come,
and I will dwell in the midst of thee, saith the Lord.
9:9 Rejoice greatly … shout …
behold, thy King cometh unto thee: he is just, and having
salvation; lowly, and riding upon an ass, and upon a colt
the foal of an ass.

MARK

11:9 And they that went before, and they
that followed, cried, saying, Hosanna; Blessed is he that
cometh in the name of the Lord:
10 Blessed be the kingdom
of our father David, that cometh in the name of the Lord:
Hosanna in the highest.

LUKE

2:10 And the angel said unto them,
Fear not: for behold, I bring you good tidings
of great joy, which shall be to all people.
13 And suddenly there was with the angel
a multitude of the heavenly host praising God, and saying,
14 Glory to God in the highest,
and on earth peace, good will toward men.
20 And the shepherds returned, glorifying
and praising God for all the things that they had heard
and seen, as it was told unto them.
6:22 Blessed are ye, when men shall hate you,
and when they shall separate you from their company, and shall
reproach you, and cast out your name as evil,
for the Son of man's sake.
23 Rejoice ye in that day, and leap for joy:
for, behold, your reward is great in heaven: for in the
like manner did their fathers unto the prophets.
10:20 ... Rejoice, because your names are written in heaven.

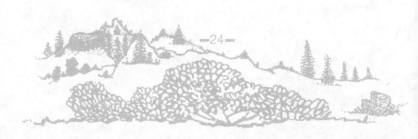

17:15 And one of them, when he saw that he was
healed, turned back, and with a loud voice glorified God,
16 And fell down on his face at his
feet, giving him thanks: and he was a Samaritan.
19:37 And when he was come nigh,
even now at the descent of the mount of Olives,
the whole multitude of the disciples began to rejoice
and praise God with a loud voice for all the mighty works
that they had seen;
38 Saying, Blessed be the King
that cometh in the name of the Lord: peace in heaven,
and glory in the highest.
24:52 And they worshipped him,
and returned to Jerusalem with great joy:
53 And were continually in the
temple, praising and blessing God.

ACTS

2:26 Therefore did my heart rejoice,
and my tongue was glad; moreover also my flesh
shall rest in hope:
28 Thou has made known to me the ways of
life; thou shalt make me full of joy with thy countenance.
46 And they, continuing daily with one accord
in the temple, and breaking bread from house to house, did
eat their meat with gladness and singleness of heart.
5:41 And they departed from the presence
of the council, rejoicing that they were counted worthy
to suffer shame for his name.
16:25 And at midnight Paul and Silas prayed,
and sang praises unto God: and the prisoners heard them.

ROMANS

4:20 He staggered not at the promise
of God through unbelief; but was strong in faith,
giving glory to God;
21 And being fully persuaded that,
what he had promised, he was able also to perform.
8:28 And we know that all things
work together for good to them that love God, to them who are the
called according to his purpose.
11:33 O the depth of the riches both
of the wisdom and knowledge of God! how unsearchable are
his judgments, and his ways past finding out!
34 For who hath known the mind
of the Lord? or who hath been his counselor?

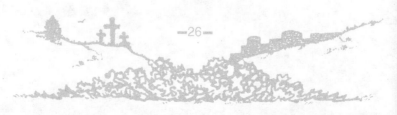

36 For of him, and through him, and
to him, are all things: to whom be glory for ever. Amen.
15:6 That ye may with one mind and one mouth
glorify God, even the Father of our Lord Jesus Christ.
13 Now the God of hope fill you
with all joy and peace in believing, that ye may abound
in hope, through the power of the Holy Spirit.

II CORINTHIANS

4:15 For all things are for your sakes,
that the abundant grace might through the thanksgiving
of many redound to the glory of God.
17 These troubles and sufferings of ours
are, after all, quite small and won't last very long.
Yet this short time of distress will result in God's richest
blessing upon us for ever and for ever (TLB).
18 So we do not look at what we can see
right now, the troubles all around us, but we look forward
to the joys in heaven which we have not yet seen.
The troubles will soon be over,
but the joys to come will last forever (TLB).
7:4 Great is my boldness of speech toward you,
great is my glorying of you: I am filled with comfort,
I am exceeding joyful in all our tribulation.

12:9 And he said unto me, My grace
is sufficient for thee: for my strength is made perfect
in weakness. Most gladly therefore will I rather glory
(find joy in) in my infirmities, that the power of Christ
may rest upon me.
10 Therefore I take pleasure
in infirmities, in reproaches, in necessities,
in persecutions, in distresses for Christ's sake:
for when I am weak, then am I strong.

EPHESIANS

3:20 Now unto him that is able to do
exceeding abundantly above all that we ask or think,
according to the power that worketh in us.
5:18 … be filled with the Spirit;
19 Speaking to yourselves in psalms
and hymns and spiritual songs, singing and making melody
in your heart to the Lord;
20 Giving thanks always for all things unto
God and the Father in the name of our Lord Jesus Christ.

PHILLIPIANS

4:6 Be careful (anxious) for nothing;
but in every thing by prayer and supplication with
thanksgiving let your requests be made known unto God.

7 And the peace of God,
which passeth all understanding, shall keep your hearts
and minds through Christ Jesus.
8 Finally, brethren, whatsoever things
are true, whatsoever things are honest, whatsoever
things are just, whatsoever things are pure, whatsoever
things are lovely, whatsoever things are of good report;
if there be any virtue, and if there be any praise,
think on these things.

COLOSSIANS

2:7 Rooted and built up in him,
and established in the faith, as ye have been taught,
filled with thanksgiving.
3:15 And let the peace of God rule in
your hearts, to the which also ye are called in one body;
and be ye thankful.
17 And whatsoever ye do in word or deed,
do all in the name of the Lord Jesus, giving thanks
to God and the Father by him.

I THESSALONIANS

5:16 Rejoice evermore.
18 In every thing give thanks: for this
is the will of God in Christ Jesus concerning you.

I TIMOTHY

2:1 I exhort therefore, that, first of all,
supplications, prayers, intercessions, and giving of thanks,
be made for all men.

HEBREWS

10:34 For ye had compassion of me
in my bonds, and took joyfully the spoiling of your goods,
knowing in yourselves that ye have in heaven a better
and an enduring substance.
13:15 By him therefore let us
offer the sacrifice of praise to God continually, that is,
the fruit of our lips giving thanks to his name.

JAMES

1:2 ... is your life full of difficulties
and temptations? Then be happy, for when the way is rough, your
patience has a chance to grow (TLB).

I PETER

2:9 But ye are a chosen generation ...
that ye should shew forth the praise of him who hath
called you out of darkness into his marvelous light.

I JOHN

1:4 And these things write we
unto you, that your joy may be full.

JUDE

1:24 Now unto him that is able to keep you
from falling, and to present you faultless before the
presence of his glory with exceeding joy,
25 ... be glory and majesty,
dominion and power, both now and ever. Amen.

REVELATION

7:11 And all the angels stood round
about the throne, and about the elders and the four
beasts, and fell before the throne on their faces,
and worshipped God,
12 Saying, Amen: Blessing, and glory,
and wisdom, and thanksgiving, and honour, and power, and
might, be unto our God for ever and ever. Amen.
11:16 And the four and twenty elders,
which sat before God on their seats, fell upon their
faces, and worshipped God,
17 Saying, We give thee thanks,
O Lord God Almighty, which art, and wast, and art to
come; because thou hast taken to thee thy great power,
and hast reigned.

19:5 And a voice came out of the throne,
saying, Praise our God, all ye his servants, and ye that
fear him, both small and great.
6 And I heard as it were the voice
of a great multitude, and as the voice of many waters,
and as the voice of mighty thunderings, saying, Alleluia:
for the Lord God omnipotent reigneth.

*Present emphasis on praise is part
of the fulfillment of these closing verses. You will be
part of this "voice of thunderings" as you share
this booklet with many other people.*

CONCLUSION

May God richly bless you as you learn and as you practice
His praise. If *The Bible on Praise* has been of some special
blessing to you, consider sending it as a greeting card for
birthdays, special greetings, Christmas cards or on other
special occasions.